LADYBUGS

by Liza Jacobs

BLACKBIRCH®
PRESS

San Diego • Detroit • New York • San Francisco • Cleveland • New Haven, Conn. • Waterville, Maine • London • Munich

© 2003 by Blackbirch Press™. Blackbirch Press™ is an imprint of The Gale Group, Inc., a division of Thomson Learning, Inc.

Blackbirch Press™ and Thomson Learning™ are trademarks used herein under license.

For more information, contact
The Gale Group, Inc.
27500 Drake Rd.
Farmington Hills, MI 48331-3535
Or you can visit our Internet site at http://www.gale.com

Photographs © 1996 by Chen Jen-Hsiang

Cover photograph © Corbis

Illustrations © 1996 by Tuei Li-Jun

© 1996 by Chin-Chin Publications Ltd.

No. 274-1, Sec.1 Ho-Ping E. Rd., Taipei, Taiwan, R.O.C.
Tel: 886-2-2363-3486 Fax: 886-2-2363-6081

LIBRARY OF CONGRESS CATALOGING-IN-PUBLICATION DATA

Jacobs, Liza.
  Ladybugs / by Liza Jacobs.
     v. cm. -- (Wild wild world)
  Contents: A ladybug is a type of beetle -- Ladybug food -- Mating -- Many kinds.
  ISBN 1-4103-0041-2
  1. Ladybugs--Juvenile literature. [1. Ladybugs.] I. Title. II. Series.

  QL596.C65J34 2003
  595.76'9--dc21
                                        2003001485

Table of Contents

About Ladybugs

A ladybug is a type of beetle. There are more than 4,000 kinds of ladybugs. They are black, brown, orange, yellow, or red. Most ladybugs have spots. Like other insects, ladybugs have two pairs of wings and six legs. They have sticky pads on their legs that help them climb.

5

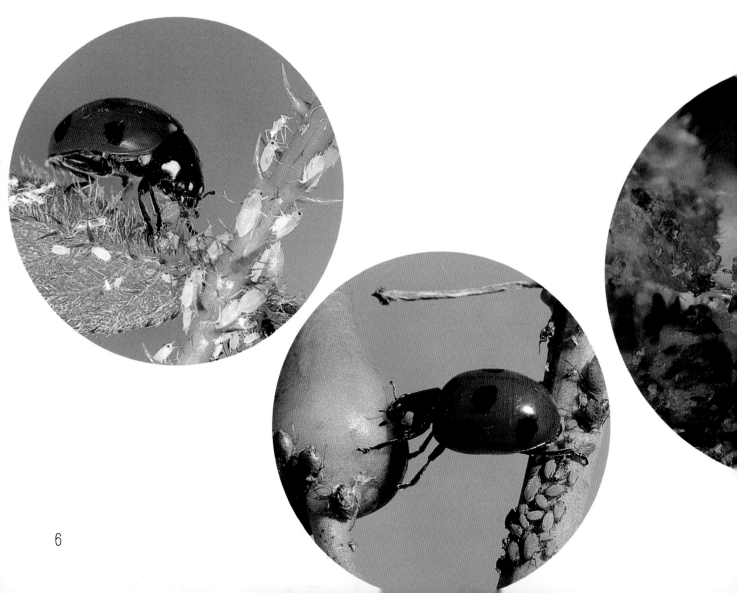

Food

Some ladybugs eat leaves, but most are meat-eaters. They eat other insects. Tiny green or red bugs called aphids are one of a ladybug's favorite foods.

Ladybugs have sensitive feet. They also have antennae on their heads. Their feet and antennae help them sense the movement of nearby insects. Once a ladybug catches a bug, it uses its strong jaws to munch its meal.

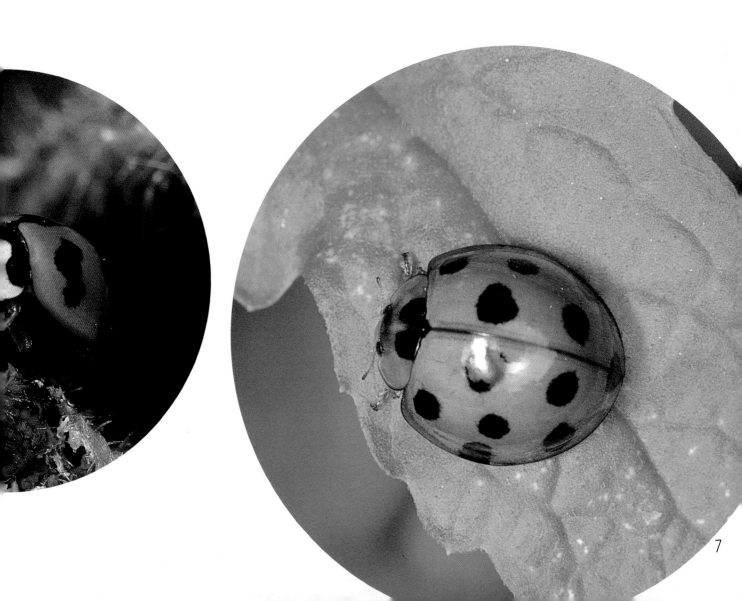

Ladybug Defenses

There are not many animals that eat ladybugs. Ladybugs have ways of staying safe. They will play dead to avoid an attack. A ladybug turns on its back and folds up its legs. When the danger has passed, it turns back over and crawls away.

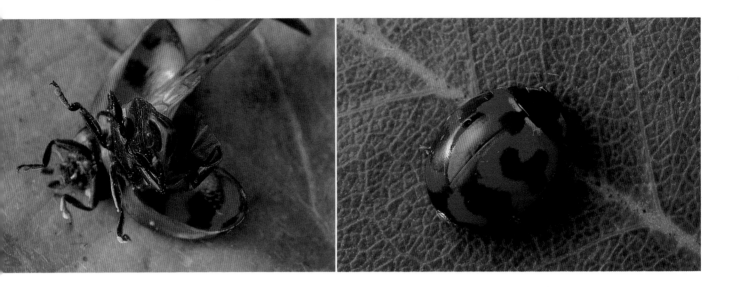

Ladybugs also have a secret weapon. They can ooze orange-colored blood from their legs! This blood has a bitter, awful taste. Most creatures that get a mouthful of ladybug blood learn to keep away from them. The bright color of a ladybug acts as a warning signal. It warns enemies of the ladybug's bad taste. Certain spiders don't seem to mind the taste. They eat ladybugs anyway. Here, a ladybug is stuck in a sticky spider web.

Finding Shelter

In warm weather, ladybugs are very active. When the weather turns colder, food is harder to find. Many kinds of ladybugs begin to settle in for the winter. They find shelter under rocks, logs, and leaves. They even crawl inside houses.

Ladybugs often gather in large groups. Sometimes millions of ladybugs can be found huddled together! They stay warm and still throughout the winter.

Mating

Ladybugs become active again when the warm spring weather returns. To make new ladybugs, they mate in the spring. Male and female ladybugs use smell and touch to find each other. The male climbs onto the back of the female to mate. Mating can take a few hours, or a few days.

Eggs

A female lays 2 to 50 bright yellow, oval eggs about a week after mating. She lays her eggs on the underside of a leaf. The female does not stay to raise her young. But she does help them survive. The spot she chooses for her eggs is always near a source of food. This way, the young can start eating as soon as they hatch.

Larvae (Lar•vah)

Ladybug eggs only take 4 or 5 days to hatch. The young are called larvae. They do not have wings or look anything like adult ladybugs—yet. But that soon changes.

Just like adult ladybugs, larvae eat insects. They like aphids, mealybugs, and other insects. Larvae will even eat each other! Larvae grow quickly and need to eat a lot of food to keep up their energy.

Molting and Changing

Insects have a hard covering over their bodies that does not grow as the insect gets larger. Instead, an insect sheds its covering as it gets bigger. This is called molting. Most ladybug larvae molt three times. The orange pattern on a larva's back begins to show after its second molt.

After about a month, a larva develops into a pupa. This is the next step as the insect changes into its adult form.

First, a larva attaches its back end to a leaf or stem with its head hanging down.

The next step in the insect's life is changing into the adult form of a ladybug.

Its body begins to get shorter and thicker as it molts one more time.

Into a Ladybug

It can take 5 days to 2 weeks for a pupa to become a ladybug. The adult ladybug forms inside the pupa. When the ladybug is ready to come out, the pupa shell splits open.

These pictures show a fully formed adult wriggling out of the pupa shell. In picture #4 the adult almost falls to the ground. It then turns itself around and climbs onto the shell in picture #5. Then the ladybug continues to crawl away. The ladybug is stretching its back wings out in picture #6.

A ladybug is pale and soft when it first comes out of the pupa stage. It does not have any spots or other markings. These develop within a few days. The ladybug's body darkens and hardens over the next few weeks.

1

2

8

3

4

6

5

Many Colors and Patterns

There are thousands of different kinds of ladybugs in a variety of colors. Some are marked with only two spots, while others have many. There are also ladybugs with other kinds of patterns.

▲ 七星瓢蟲

People often like ladybugs because they are pretty to look at. They also help people by eating pests that ruin gardens and farm crops. Ladybugs are a wonderful part of our natural world.

For More Information

Hartley, Karen and Macro, Chris. *Ladybug.* Des Plaines, IL: Heinemann Library, 1998.

Johnson, Sylvia A. *Ladybugs.* Minneapolis, MN: Lerner Publications, 1983.

Pascoe, Elaine. *Beetles (Nature Close-Up Series).* San Diego, CA: Blackbirch Press, 2001

Ross, Michael Elsohn. *Ladybugology.* Minneapolis, MN: Carolrhoda Books, 1997.

Glossary

larva the young that hatches from a ladybug egg

molt to shed the outer skin or covering

pupa the stage between larva and adult